To Kenneth —
who knows traditions

Without Warning

of the family
of poeting + traveling!
Here are my latest poems.
With all best wishes
for all your endeavors."

Jay
11/26/18

Without Warning

The Marrakech Poems
by
Fay Picardi

Burnt Umber Press
2018

Copyright © 2017 Fay Picardi

Art Copyright © 2017 Cindy Michaud

Kathy Garvey, Book Editor
David Richardson, Poetry Editor

Cover design by Kathy Garvey.
Cover photo of Madrasa Ben Youssef
by Fay Picardi.
Border design and formatting by Kathy Garvey.

All rights reserved.

Rumi quotation is from "Great Wagon" in *The Essential Rumi: New Expanded Edition Translations*. Copyright 2004 by Coleman Barks. Permission granted by Mr. Barks.

Quotations by Albert Einstein on page 31 and T.S. Eliot on page 69 fall within Fair Use guidelines.

For Marrakech and certain other Arabic words and locales, the author has chosen to use the French spelling.

ISBN-13:9781727098938
ISBN-10:1727098935

*For my grandchildren,
Jack, Maddie, Will and Mac,
with every hope that they will always
explore, respect and appreciate
other cultures and other beliefs.*

OUT BEYOND IDEAS
OF WRONGDOING AND
RIGHTDOING
THERE IS A FIELD.
I WILL MEET YOU
THERE.

Jalaluddin Mevlana Rumi
(1207-1273)

Contents

The Red City
Amur AKush — 3

The Call to Prayer
Fajr — 9
Dhuhr — 11
Ash — 13
Maghrib — 15
Isla'a — 17

The Medina
Burnt Sienna — 21
The Art of Transformation — 25
Lorenzo's Giraffe — 29
In the Souks — 33
Moroccan Lanterns — 37
Hide and Seek — 39

In the Gardens of Marrakech
The Secret Garden — 43
In the Garden of Yves Saint Laurent — 45
Three Times the Charm — 47

The High Atlas Mountains
Inheritance — 53
What Has Not Been Lost — 55
Alchemy — 57

Departures
What We Do Not See — 61
Ras el Hanout — 63
Hajj — 65

The Red City

Amur A Kush
(City of God)

In the evening sun,
the ramparts of Marrakech
deceive the mind.
The rosy hue of the walls,
a sienna ribbon
weaving in and out,
is an intrigue.
Low towers.
Ornate and arched gateways
to an unknown world.

Must I accuse you, Yusef ibn Tachufin?
You used your slaves
(almost a thousand years ago)
to build your wall.
To assure your kingdom.
Berber that you were.

Next you followed the call of Islam
and conquered Spain.

What you could not conquer
were the souls of your own mountain people.
Or the passions of your desert tribes.

Trace the sunset glow
against the sandstone bricks.
Skirt the inner mysteries,
daring your mind to understand.

Who among us has found
a soul's sanctuary?
A place within ourselves,
impenetrable by time, or fear.

> # The Call to Prayer

I

Fajr
(Dawn to Sunrise)

First ray of light
and over the city, a sound
clearer than the ringing of a crystal bell.

More pure
than the trickle of spring water
from the mountains.

Deeper
than the flutter of morning doves
above low rooftops.

A chant that gives birth to the day.
That gives words
to a reason for living.

Allah, God, Jehovah.
Listen and be humbled.

II

Dhuhr
(Just after True Noon)

Intonations waft
from the minarets.
No need to know
what words are said.
If we agree or not.

A hush accompanies their flight
above the braziers, the bakeries, the cafés.
Mingling with the smoke
and smell of tagine and couscous,
the quiet tells us what we need to know.

Faith can come
in many senses,
floating down to touch
that part of us
we least understand.

III

Ash
(Afternoon)

Inside the city walls,
the shadows are starting their artistry.
Muted colors begin to creep
onto streets
and up eastern edifices
offering passersby shelter from the sun.

The arched entries to mosques,
schools, the Souks
tease with geometric shapes
that play hide and seek
with light and dark.

From minarets,
the reassuring voice of a Muezzin
resounds over riads, small offices, stores.
In multi-colored djellaba,
the faithful kneel on straw mats.
Face Mecca. Become prostrate.
The streets are awash in brilliance.

In the High Atlas Mountains beyond,
in the Western Sahara below,
everywhere, the sounds of supplication.
Despite the recent tumult of daily living,
for a few minutes, over all,
a discernible stillness descends.

IV

Maghrib
(Evening between Twilight and Dark)

As if some genie has escaped
from his bottle,
the calls from the minarets
pass over the city
and with them, the smoke,
the smells from a thousand fires.

The day merchants are folding their tents
and packing away their wares.
The Jamma el-Fna Square is alive
with the coming of night.
In the food stalls, the fires are lit
beneath kebob and tagine.
The magicians and musicians
have unpacked their instruments.

At the first word of the call,
all activity ceases.

Twilight provides a place for prayer,
leading some into a time of reflection.
Others into the boisterous night.

V

Isla'a
(Night)

Give thanks that you are human
for this is the time of poets.
Or the time for reciting poems.
This is the time for the touch
of whispered words on rooftops
or in dark passageways.

Inside,
there is a coolness,
perhaps low talk or laughter.
Quiet movement from pillar to pillar.
Shadows instruct everywhere.

The courtyard pool sparkles
a constellation of stars.
Sometimes a moon.

Give over to your god
the rewards and worries of the day.
Prepare for sleep.

The Medina

Burnt Sienna

In the Medina,
seduction awaits with every turn.
Reach out and touch
the towering walls,
somehow soft and alluring
in the morning sun.
They offer themselves to you
for the touching.

Follow the square grey tiles,
uneven and ancient,
down the narrow path.
They entice
the imagination.

Further and further
into the labyrinth.

Here and there a door,
solid and unrevealing,
increases the mystery.

Unyielding walls ahead
make turning left or right a game
until there is no longer
any choice of turning.

Imagine traveling this maze at dusk.
Heart pounding above the rattle of a wooden cart
pulled, not by donkeys, but by two men
with two more alongside.

No foreboding, no premonitions,
just ominous allure
and a great deal of palpitation.

In the day light,
there is evidence of other life.
A small boy with his older brother
kicks a ball from side to side,
silent in the narrow lane.
(The Qurän says we must not
disturb our neighbors.)
Before a door,
a servant caught at her sweeping
shrinks into the shadows.
(Cleanliness pleases Allah.)
A housewife, nodding and shy,
hurries home with her produce.
(Modesty is becoming to Allah.)

All over the Medina,
pathways meander.
No need to know where you are going.
The tease is enough.

Come with me.
Let's be flagstone nomads.
There are so many ways to be seduced.
Don't be coy.
You already know your preferences.

The Art of Transformation
(Madrasa Ben Youssef)

Walk with me
quietly down a long corridor
lit by filigree lanterns
and filled with reverent whispers.
Take a sharp right—
one always turns right—
every shopkeeper knows this.
Pass through the arches
and, suddenly, a majestic world.
A courtyard, a pool,
a thousand designs so intertwined
they make a whole.

Here in the Madrasa Ben Youssef
for nearly three hundred years,
thousands of students, all male,
answered the Call to Prayer.
Faced Mecca five times a day.
Returned to their Quränic studies.
Pursued enlightenment.

In small cells, they watched the light
from the sky above
and its reflection from the pool below
enter through the minute patterns
of carved screens.

Stand beside me.
See tiles so intricate, colors so intimate,
they evoke another world.
Arches, squares, octagons,
flowing script from the prophets.
So repetitive, so hypnotic,
the mind is seduced
and travels to another sphere.

No images of the living here.
No plants, no animals, no humans.
Only precise beauty.
And the admiration of beauty.

Lorenzo's Giraffe

Creativity is more important than knowledge.
                                        Albert Einstein

1

With her gentle brown eyes,
Lorenzo dei Medici's Egyptian giraffe
astounds all Florence.
Her grace and beauty,
her ornamentations
mesmerize.
Even the Sultan who sent her
(in exchange, of course, for other bounty)
could not have imagined
the power she would bestow.

2

Against the ornate arches
outside the Madrasa Ben Youssef,
an old woman sits in the dust
surrounded by her coarse covering skirt.
The small hand-sewn giraffes she is offering
are scattered about her like flowers.
A plethora of pigments.
(She has chosen the most vibrant leather scraps.)
Each of her creations is painted
with perfectly placed white polka-dots.

3

In Miss Maggie's garden,
a little girl creates ballroom beauties.
From opening buds,
she makes their ruffled headdresses.
From full blooms,
she fashions their multicolored skirts.
Hollyhock belles billow about her
as she sits in the sunshine.
Their festivities delight
even the most uninitiated passersby.
She knows nothing of giraffes.

In the Souks

Memory is a funny thing.
What comes back
and what doesn't.
How certain scenes emerge,
then recede
only to emerge again.

In the Souks, what waits
in the shadows
is intrigue.
All the fantasies
one could ever dream of
or hear.

But what emerges
is a truth you can count on.
Or is it the opposite?

Here is a story.
Only a simple story.
Not long, but important.

There once was a man
who sold leather goods
in a shop not six feet wide.
A humble man, and quiet.
One who did not call out, or follow.
Or even try to persuade.

Still, he surprised me.

"Madame. Madame,"
he whispered
in a voice which might
have caused recoil.

He held out the money
I had just given him.

"You have paid too much.
This is a euro note, worth ten times
the cost of your purchase. Please.
Would you do me the honor
of giving me the correct amount?"

Only a simple story.
Not long, but important.

Moroccan Lanterns

I don't know much
about this business of darkness and light.
Why we sometimes see stars in daylight
where there are none at night.
Even fireflies in a glass jar can astound.
First, the darkness. Then the flurry of light.

Old Moroccan lanterns—
new ones, too—
capture the imagination.
Through colored stones
and geometric shapes cut into metal,
they disperse tiny sparks of essence
into time and distance.
Little universes glowing
on walls, on floors.
On faces.

Inner light, divine light, white light.
Let there be light, a baptism of light.
As some believe, God is light.

How little we know.

Hide and Seek

No need to knock.
The door to the Garden of Eden is opened to us.
A smiling Eve (Ukrainian, she says, and chic)
ushers us into an oasis.
A courtyard of gigantic palms.
Couples disguised in the dimness.
All around, elaborate objects,
exotic smells mix East with West,
old with new.
Istanbul in the Twenties? Paris?

How did we arrive here?
A few lighthearted artists
traveling through streets
now emptied of their merchants.
Wares and shops folded back into the night.
Doors closed.
Only stucco walls and paving stones
to echo our merriment.

Who laughs or loves or argues
behind these wooden doors?

Door. Wall. War.
How can a single word hold such meaning?
The joy and suffering are endless.

Language is a funny thing.
It has been scientifically documented
(you must have heard)
words alone can control us.

In the Gardens of Marrakech

The Secret Garden

A play of light along green tiles
shimmers deepest, darkest jade.
Green, green waves these tiles become,
these pathways leading out
in four cardinal directions.

Follow them from the source, the center.
Sink into the beauty
of this most enticing sea,
glistening through scented meadows.
Smell rosemary and garlic
and flowering jasmine.

Outside these garden walls,
there is a small narrow street
full of noise, the business of daily life.

Inside, only the Garden of Eden.
A breeze through ornamental grasses.
The soft bubbling sound of a spring
flowing underground from the mountains
to the center, to its fountain
which cradles the songs of birds.

Here is tranquility.
Here is symmetry.
A studied plan that rests the eye.
That opens the soul.

In the Garden of Yves Saint Laurent
(The Majorelle Gardens)

Green.
Palms, palmettos, bamboo
give grace here. Shelter from the sun.

Cobalt.
And convincing.
It surprises in fountains, on walls,
in the tile of man-made streams.

Cadmium yellow.
Flower pots, window grills
mimic the sun in their brilliance.

An artist's paradise.
Here, a young girl bends over her sketchbook.
There, a photographer aims his lens at a leaf.
Beyond, an aspirant works paint onto a canvas.

The painter who spent years planning this garden,
the designer whose creations make it famous,
both still inhabit its luxuriance.
Here, they have captured Marrakech
and condensed it into pure palette.
A world within a world,
where being is more important,
even,
than beauty.

Three Times the Charm
(Mint Tea)

A sparkling, a smell,
a steaming stream of sweet.
A three foot waterfall of amber
in the noonday light.
Already we are absorbed
into the ritual,
captured by the repetition,
mesmerized by the precise pour
of Moroccan Mint Tea.

Oh, yes. Be assured.
There are threes.
There must be threes.
In art.
In religion.
Trinity, triumvirate, triad.
And here before us at the Hotel Mamounia,
three pots, three pours, three cups of tea.

How much we share,
we who believe in a Supreme Being,
who pray for peace, and love.
And even comfort
for *all* the people of the world.

Now is the time for thanks.
Here in this place, at this time,
while the silver pot is heated
and the tea leaves are steeped.
While the Nana mint
is readied for the pour.

Three times.
Three different tastes.

Some things do not change.
Not in the Maghrebi.
Not in the rest of the world.
In each of us who believe
there remains a glimmer,
sometimes almost made invisible,
a tiny sparkle in the stream.

The High Atlas Mountains

Inheritance

More than 1,600 miles
of Atlas Mountain peaks
shelter the Berber peoples
as they carry their stories
from village to village
on rocky footpaths,
across ridges, and time.

For five thousand years, they have continued
to turn what little they have been given
into a richness of life and art.

Here there is no desert yet.
Only a wild and barren beauty
of rock and stream.
Of small trees. Small animals.

Here streambeds climb higher and higher.
The sound grows louder and louder
until it covers, and hushes,
all human speech.

Here, at the source, a waterfall.
The spray—
the taste of it on the tongue,
the touch of it on the skin,
the sight of the leaping, tumbling power of it,
the smell of pine trees it carries through the air,
all make easy remembering
what treasures we have been given.

Why we must mourn even the smallest theft.

What Has Not Been Lost

From these hills,
the North African Elephant
has long ago disappeared.
(Ah, what stories have been told!
Of war and winning. Of defeat.
Of Hannibal, Caesar, Cleopatra.)

The Barbary Bear
(despite the rumors)
was last seen a hundred years ago.

The Barbary Lion
(the largest in the world
and the most fierce)
has recently become extinct.

From among the wild ones,
only the Barbary Leopard remains,
diminished but proud.

The Berber women, too, remain.
They provide. They nourish. They sustain.
As strong and wizened as the ancient argon trees
whose roots protect them from the drought,
these women repopulate the disappearing trees.
They plant seedlings, tend saplings,
hold back with their deep roots
the encroaching desert.

Alchemy

One old lady,
among a select few.
Seated.
Turning a grindstone.

Slowly.
Slowly, she crushes the nuts,
as attentive as if creating the soil
from which the world will be formed.

Stone on stone
until the essence of time
appears grain by grain
from the nuts she is grinding.

What she produces is a paste,
ready to be pummeled
into that liquid gold
called Argon Oil
to which some ascribe miracles.

Departures

What We Do Not See

Brilliantly colored spices
explode like fireworks
from the spice stalls of Jamma el-Fna.
These horizontal rainbows
whet the imagination of poets and artists,
all manner of esthetes.

Such an exotic display
gives no hint of dirt or toil.
The hours of planting, plucking, drying, sorting.
The feeding of donkeys, the repair of carts.
(And such a poor pittance in return.)

In our delight, we are imagining
the myriad of spices we will carry home
along with hand-painted tagine pots.

What we are seeing are not spices.
We are seeing a cornucopia of cones
made from cardboard,
rolled in glue
and covered in dyed grains.

We ignore the deception.

What we do not see
tells the real story.

Ras el Hanout
(The Shopkeeper's Mix)

I have always believed in genetic memory.
Science has taken decades to prove me right.
Olfactory memory is so much easier to confirm.
You can do it yourself.

No need to be told that smell
connects to areas of the brain
that trigger emotion and memory.
Just think of popcorn or the scent of smoke.

Give me the aroma of maple syrup
and I am back in my grandmother's kitchen,
tiny and warm, eating pancakes.

So it is with the shopkeeper's mix.
One whiff of cinnamon,
cumin or ginger, turmeric or saffron
and I am standing in front of a spice stall
in the Jamma el-Fna square,
remembering the smell of roasting lamb.

I have saved a little Ras el Hanout.
Shall I prepare a feast for us?
I'll make a lamb tagine.
While it simmers, we can sit together.
Share memories.

Hajj

Islamic architecture intrigues me.
Its intricacies. Its histories.
And how the complexities of any faith
reflect a belief in the Divine.

Think of Mecca.
Follow the pilgrims inside the walls
and watch as they circle the sacred Kaaba,
said to be the very temple
built centuries ago over the altar of Adam.

Round and round the faithful circle,
each time trying to kiss the Black Stone,
shrouded in silver, sacred.
Given by Allah to Abraham and Ishmael.

Five days. Five pillars of Islam.

Faith is so hard to understand.
Mormon, Christian, Jewish, Islamic.
All.
Many names. One God.

But let us begin our pilgrimage.
Who knows where it will lead us.

> "We shall not cease from exploration
> And the end of all our exploring
> Will be to arrive where we started
> And know the place for the first time."

From *Little Gidding*
Four Quartets
by T.S. Eliot

Acknowledgments

My many, many thanks go to the following:

My editor extraordinaire, David Richardson, for the many hours of editing, discussing and advising he has dedicated to this volume. Working together has been a joyful journey.

My friend and fellow adventurer, Kathy Garvey, without whose skills of formatting and editing, the existence and exceptional quality of this volume and my other books would not have been possible.

My friend and travel companion, Cindy Michaud, whose art from our trip together to Morocco informs my poetry and whose pen and ink drawing inspired by the Madrasa Ben Youssef appears in this book.

And finally, my husband, John Picardi, my Napoleon's Corporal, whose encouragement, support and feed-back help me pursue my passion for traveling, writing and publishing.

Biographies

Fay Picardi is an internationally published poet and author of three volumes of poetry as well as a historical novel. She loves art, travel and learning about almost anything, especially other cultures and religions. Her work draws from her childhood in Kentucky, her year in France as a young teacher and her frequent travels to Europe, often to France and Italy. She has two daughters and four grandchildren. When not traveling, she lives in Florida with her husband.

Kathy Garvey is a graphic designer/fabric artist living in Palm Bay, Florida. She is also the editor, resident artist and publishing specialist for Burnt Umber Press.

Cindy Michaud currently lives and works in the western mountains of North Carolina. She enjoys travel adventures as well as art and is happiest when the two intersect. When not traveling, she is in her studio creating art across a broad spectrum of media and publishing a blog every Friday.

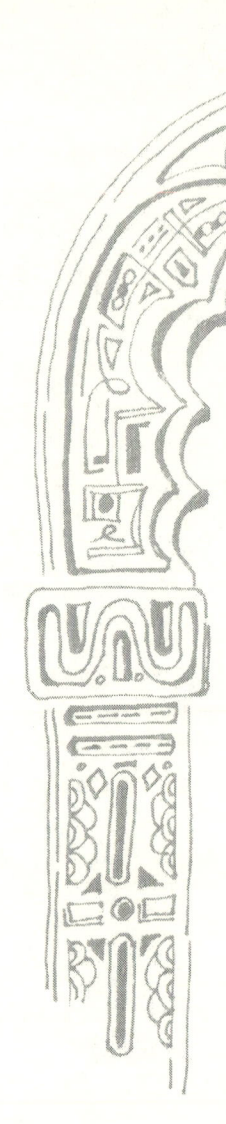

More...

You can learn more about Fay Picardi at www.faypicardi.weebly.com.
The following books are available at Amazon.com. Search Fay Picardi.

Nana's Sunday Dance (Poetry)
The Stones Speak with Cindy Michaud (Poetry and Art)
Without Warning with Cindy Michaud (Poetry and Art)
Simonetta (Historical Novel) an exploration into the extraordinary life of Simonetta Vespucci, Botticelli's muse and inspiration for his *The Birth of Venus*.

Kathy Garvey has an Etsy shop featuring her fabric art and watercolors at www.etsy.com/shop/SnailFlower.

Enjoy more of Cindy Michaud's art work at: www.cindymichaud.com or contact her at art@cindymichaud.com.

Cindy, Fay and Kathy are all members of the painting group Pieces of 8:
http://piecesof8art.blogspot.com/.